3 1994 01138 9597

SANTA ANA PUBLIC LIBRARY

AR PTS: 1.0

D0579515

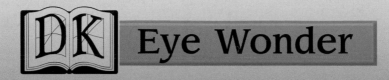

DK Eye Wonder

Birds

J 598 GRA
Gray, Samantha
Birds

MCFADDEN

$17.95
31994011389597

LONDON, NEW YORK, MUNICH,
MELBOURNE AND DELHI

Written and edited by
Samantha Gray and Sarah Walker
Designed by Mary Sandberg,
Cathy Chesson, and Jacqueline Gooden

Managing editor Sue Leonard
Managing art editor Rachael Foster
US editors Margaret Parrish and Gary Werner
Jacket design Chris Drew
Picture researchers
Marie Osborn and Sarah Pownall
Production Kate Oliver
DTP designer Almudena Díaz
Consultant Mark Fox

First American Edition 2002

02 03 04 05 06 07 08 09 10 9 8 7 6 5 4 3 2 1

Published in the United States by
DK Publishing, Inc.
95 Madison Avenue
New York, NY 10016

Copyright © 2002 Dorling Kindersley Limited

All rights reserved under International and Pan-American Copyright
Conventions. No part of this publication may be reproduced, stored in a retrieval
system, or transmitted in any form or by any means, electronic, mechanical,
photocopying, recording, or otherwise, without the prior written permission of
the copyright owner. Published in Great Britain by Dorling Kindersley Limited.

DK publishing offers special discounts for bulk purchases for sales promotions
or premiums. Specific, large-quantity needs can be met with special editions,
including personalized covers, excerpts of existing guides, and corporate
imprints. For more information, contact Special Markets Department, DK
Publishing Inc., 95 Madison Avenue, New York, NY 10016 Fax: 800-600-9098.

A catalog record for this book is available from the Library of Congress

ISBN 0-7894-8550-8 ISBN 0-7894-8551-6 (ALB)

Color reproduction by Colourscan, Singapore
Printed and bound Italy by L.E.G.O.
see our complete
product line at
www.dk.com

Contents

What is a bird?

There are about 9,000 different species of birds living on Earth, and all evolved from reptiles millions of years ago. Birds live in almost every part of the world, from the icy Antarctic to steamy tropical rain forests.

Birds have wings instead of arms.

Birds have a strong horny beak and no teeth.

Lightweight skeleton

This is a crow's skeleton. As with all flying birds, its bones are hollow, like straws. Solid bones would make birds too heavy to fly.

This bird bone has a honeycomb structure.

Wishbone

Ulna, a wing bone.

Scaly toes and feet.

On the inside

Birds cannot chew food as they do not have any teeth. Instead they have a special grinding organ called a gizzard, which is a part of the stomach. Food is crushed as it passes through the gizzard.

The keel anchors the wing muscles.

The ankle bone.

Fancy flier

As with all birds of prey, this red-tailed hawk is a powerful flyer. The wings are large and strong, allowing the hawk to fly and soar for many hours at a time. Wing shape and size varies hugely between bird species.

Down feather

Body feather

Flight feather

Useful feathers

Feathers are essential for flight, but they also keep birds warm, act as camouflage, and can be used in mating displays. Each bird has several different types of feathers, including down, body, and flight feathers.

Almost too small to see!

The tiny bee hummingbird weighs only 0.05 oz (1.6 g), and is smaller than some insects in its rain forest home. The largest bird in the world is the ostrich.

Feathery facts

● There are many millions of birds living on Earth.

● Only birds, bats, and insects are capable of powered flight.

● All birds have feathers, even those that cannot fly.

The plumed whistling-duck is a waterfowl.

The stunning scarlet ibis is a wading bird.

Different birds

The many thousands of bird species are divided into specific families. The families include birds of prey, songbirds, parrots, waterfowl, and waders.

The chaffinch is a perching song bird.

5

Colorful chorus

The unusual song of male gouldian finches is made up of hisses, clicks, and long, shrill sounds. Living together in flocks, rainbow-colored gouldian finches are sociable birds.

Songbirds

Some birds sing particularly musical and enchanting songs. They are called songbirds, and the best known is the nightingale. Songbirds have a special voice box, called a syrinx, with thin walls that vibrate as they sing. In this way, they produce more complex and beautiful sounds than other birds.

Star performer

The nightingale sings loudly and musically. Its low, long notes are particularly haunting. Singing fearlessly through the day and night, the nightingale is not a shy bird.

The nightingale's special voice box allows it to sing its haunting song.

Street singer

The warbling song of European robins proclaims their territory. After pairs form to breed, only the male sings. Under streetlights, he may sing into the night.

Feathery facts

● During the breeding season, male songbirds use their song to entice females and warn away other males.

● The mockingbird can imitate snatches of songs from 20 or more other bird species, all within a few minutes!

Singing a love song

At dusk, the song thrush finds a treetop perch and delivers its powerful song. Males looking for a mate give the longest performances. They may also deliver a battle song when competing with other males.

Life at the top

Rooks' nests are likely to be built high up in a tree. These large birds tend to nest in the same tree, or nearby trees, for life, and sometimes even reuse old nests. Sociable birds, rooks like to nest close together.

Woodworkers

Many birds make their homes, and base their lives, around woodlands and forests. Nesting, feeding, and socializing can all take place in a tree. Different species of birds prefer different trees.

The drumming bird

There are many different kinds of woodpecker, all living in heavily wooded areas. Each bird pecks into a tree in order to make a home, dig out insects, and attract a mate.

Woodpeckers are able to drum on

Rooks nests sway around in high winds, so they need to be tough!

TONGUE TWISTER

Although it may be hard to spot, woodpeckers have a very long, sticky tongue! This can be up to 4 inches (10 cm) long and is used to pull insects out of trees. When not in use, the tongue is withdrawn back into the bird's head, out of the way until the next time it is needed.

...ree several thousand times a day.

Tiny nutcracker

This nuthatch has a taste for both insects and nuts. It cracks open tough nuts by wedging them into a hole on a tree branch and striking them with its beak. It makes its nest in a tree hole.

Creeping around

Treecreepers are small birds that spiral up and around tree trunks in search of insects. When their journey on one tree is complete, the birds swoop down to the bottom of another tree and continue their hunt for food.

Game birds

Traditionally bred for sport, this group of decorative birds includes grouse, pheasants, partridges, and quails. Game birds tend to be ground-dwelling, and the majority are not strong flyers.

Troop of turkeys

Wild turkeys live in areas of the US, favoring habitats that combine woodlands and open clearings. They feed mainly on plant material, although they may also snack on insects and spiders.

Spiked tail feathers form the shape of a fan.

Star turn

This male sage grouse is staging a show to impress the ladies! Each spring, males spread out their tails, puff out their necks, and utter deep bubbling noises to attract a female. She then selects a partner that she likes the look of.

Flock of pheasants
These large birds live in pairs during the breeding season and small flocks throughout the rest of the year. There are many different species of pheasants, so color and markings varies widely.

Birds of prey

Superb hunters, birds of prey have much
sharper eyesight than people. They catch pre
with their feet, swooping down to grasp their
victims. Their hooked beaks tear up the meal

American beauty

Bald eagles are the national bird of the US. They
snatch fish from just below the water's surface.
Sometimes they plunge in after their prey.
They swim using their wings before
flying off with their catch. Their
heads are snowy white, not bald.
Pairs mate for life.

*Huge wings give ospreys
their ability to soar.*

*Fish-eating birds
of prey have bare
legs so that they
don't get wet
"socks" during
a fishing trip!*

Fast fishing

Ospreys fly high over
water, diving down at high
speed to catch fish. Just before
hitting the water, they thrust their feet
forward and plunge into the water to
grab their prey. The osprey's feet feel like
sandpaper, which makes them useful for
gripping slippery fish.

Snake snack

With the longest legs of any bird of prey, the secretary bird attacks from the ground rather than the air. It uses its powerful legs to stun a snake by stamping on it. The secretary bird then kills the snake by stabbing it with its back talon before seizing it in its beak.

Tough scales on its legs protect the secretary bird from poisonous snakebites.

With its piercing eyesight, the hawk scans for prey over a wide area.

High society

Harris's hawks are unusually sociable birds of prey. They hunt in groups, working together to catch prey that has gone into cover. One bird approaches to drive it out and the others hang back, ready to chase the prey.

Amazing owls

Most owls wake up as dusk falls. They preen themselves, combing their heads with their claws. Velvety flight feathers muffle the flapping of their wings as they take to the skies. Their hoots, screeches, and whistles break the silence of the night.

Invisible owl

In woodland, owls slumber in trees during the day. Their brownish feathers blend in with the bark. This great horned owl has tufts of feathers that look like horns.

Spectacular!

Spectacled owls have markings that look like a pair of spectacles around their eyes. The young have the opposite coloring of the parents and are white with black spectacles.

As white as snow

Sometimes called Arctic owls or ghost owls, snowy owls change color with the seasons from gray-brown to white. In the snow, a white owl can sneak up on prey unseen.

Turning heads

Owls have forward-looking eyes. To see to the side or back, this barn owl must turn its head. It can swivel its head a long way around.

Swift and silent

Sweeping silently through the skies, eagle owls listen intently for small sounds. Their prey may not even hear them approach as they swoop down to sink in their talons.

Watch-and-wait hunters

Not all birds fly in search of food. Many prefer to find a perch that serves as a lookout post. There, they watch and wait. As soon as they spy their prey, they act fast to grab it. Some snap up insects in the air, while others swoop to seize them from the ground. The kingfisher even dives into rivers to catch fish.

The flycatcher eats many different kinds of insect.

Sitting and staring

The European roller's lookout perch can be anything from a branch to a telephone wire. From here, this colorful bird watches for prey.

Dragonflies are a delicious delicacy for many watch-and-wait hunters.

The art of bee-eating

The bee-eater grabs insects in midair, even eating bees and wasps! It grasps stinging insects in the tip of its beak and rubs the sting against a perch or on the ground. This squeezes out the venom or the sting itself. The insect is then safe to swallow.

Making a splash

Perched on a branch over a river or stream, kingfishers watch for fish. When they spot one, they dive after it at high speed. Before hitting the water, they fold their wings and close their eyes.

Camouflage

To escape the attention of predators, birds must be able to blend in with their surroundings. Even brightly colored birds such as parrots can be hard to spot in exotic rain forests. Other birds seem plainer, but their disguises are just as good.

Hidden in all seasons

This white-tailed ptarmigan is a master of disguise! As shown above, in the cold winter months it is a startling snowy-white. In summer its feathers change to a rich brown color. The main picture shows the bird in the fall, with a mixture of summer and winter feathers.

Life in the reeds

This hidden heron is an American bittern, and lives in swamps and marshes in the US and Canada. When threatened, the bittern will freeze with its beak pointed upward, sometimes gently swaying to blend in with the surrounding reeds and grasses.

Safe on the beach

This ringed plover knows that her eggs will be safe if they can't be spotted. A rocky section of beach is the perfect place for this wading bird to make her nest.

These eggs look just like the pebbles that surround them.

Colors of the rainbow

Hot, steamy jungles that teem with life, rain forests provide birds with a rich variety of food to feast on. Flowers bloom and produce fruit where tall trees reach the light, and the lower layers of the forest swarm with insects.

Feathered friends

Brilliantly colored manakins hide in the lush, leafy, lower branches of the rain forest. Their fast flight and small size makes them hard to spot, but there are usually lots of them!

Shake your tail feathers

On a rain forest perch, male bird of paradise display their beautifu feathers to attract mates. They rais their tail feathers over their back and tip forward to show them off This scarlet-feathere bird of paradise ma perform for hours

Flowers produce a sweet juice called nectar that hummingbirds suck through their strawlike beaks.

Toucan talk

With loud, croaking calls that sound like a frog's, toucans call to each other as they fly in search of fruit. Toucan pairs play games of catch, tossing berries to their mate.

A BIRD WITH A BIG BEAK

A toucan's beak is up to one-third the length of its body. It is so big that it seems amazing that the bird does not topple forward. In fact, the beak is hollow and lightweight. It is also useful. Toucans can pick fruit on faraway branches. They toss the fruit into the air and swallow it.

Fast flapping

Jewel-like hummingbirds beat their wings so fast that they make a humming sound. Hovering near flowers, they sink in their long beaks to suck out nectar and insects.

The parrot family

Containing more than 300 species, the parrot family includes many of the world's most beautiful and brightly colored birds. Some parrots live in dense tropical rain forests, others in large open plains.

A muddy meal

These noisy macaws have gathered on a mud bank in South America. It is thought that they peck at the soil and clay to get extra minerals that are missing from their everyday diet.

Flocks of pets

Sociable birds, budgerigars live in vast flock in Australia. Although small, budgerigar can fly vast distances in hot and dry weather in search of food and water. Wild budgerigars are always green, with a yellow face and black marking

Feathery facts

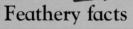

- Parrots are good climbers, using their beaks and claws to move around the branches.

- Parrots eat mainly fruit, nuts, and seeds.

- If one parrot spots food, it will alert the rest of the flock.

Finger food

Many birds grip their food with their feet, but parrots are the only birds that can hold food up to their beaks. Their fleshy toes act like human fingers!

The crested bird

Cockatoos are white, pink, or black. Their large head crests are raised when the birds are angry, excited, or frightened.

The fig is gripped tightly in this green parrot's claws.

Loving parrots

Lovebirds live up to their name, since they are fond of sitting in pairs and preening each other! All nine species originally come from Africa and nearby islands.

Rainbow colors

Parakeets are small parrots. There are many species of these birds, living in flocks in warm and tropical areas.

Wading in

Wading birds live in swamps and marshes, and along the edges of rivers and lakes. These wet areas are an ideal home to many birds, since the shallow water and soaking land are full of food.

Flat-footed wader

There are eight species of jacana, a small tropical wading bird with extremely large feet. The spidery toes allow each bird to walk on floating plants. This wattled jacana lives in Central and South America.

Silent hunter

Gray herons are superb hunters and often stand motionless in the water for hours, waiting for a fish to swim by. Their razor-sharp beak is also used to grab insects and frogs, and occasionally small mammals.

Flocks of flamingos

Flamingos always live in large flocks, and there may be many thousands of birds in one group. Although they are wading birds, flamingos are also strong swimmers and flyers.

Feathery facts

- Wading birds have long legs so that their bodies don't get wet in the water.

- Flamingos are pink because some of the food that they eat, such as plankton and algae, contains a special pigment.

- There are five species of flamingo in the world.

This flamingo is filtering food with its curved beak.

Filter feeding

Flamingos feed on tiny water creatures, which they sieve out of the mud by filtering them through their unusual, upside-down beaks. These beaks contain rows of bristles, called lamellae, which strain water.

Wonderful waterfowl

Lakes, ponds, rivers, and other freshwater areas are a
favorite place for waterfowl such as ducks, geese, and
swans to live. There are many different species of these
water-loving birds, which can be found around the world.

Life by the sea

The emperor goose lives
in ponds and marshes close
to the sea. These geese are
very noisy, communicating
frequently with the rest of
the flock. Emperor geese
eat some shellfish,
as well as grasses.

Sociable swans

Mute swans are sociable creatures, and many may live
in a small area. To begin flying, these large birds use the
water as a runway, flapping their wings and running
along the surface of the water until they finally take of

Distinguished ducks

These black-bellied whistling ducks make a very shrill
whistling sound! These vocal birds live in small flocks
and are easily recognizable with their bright pink beaks.

Feathery facts

● Most birds have between 1,500 and 3,000 feathers, but some swans can have over 25,000 feathers.

● All waterfowl have webbed feet. These act as flippers, pushing the birds through the water.

Flying female

This female mallard is brown all over, whereas the male is brighter, with a green head. The female quacks more loudly than the male.

Seabirds

Some seabirds spend most of their lives soaring over the open ocean. Others search for food on the seashore. At nesting time, most cluster together on cliffs in huge groups called colonies. With birds on every level, a cliff is like a high-rise apartment building!

Puffins and pufflings

Brightly colored beaks and black-and-white feathers give puffins a special appearance. Most of their lives are spent on the open ocean. They can swim and fly. To breed, puffins travel to rocky islands where they build their nests. Their chicks are called pufflings.

A pelican's beak holds three times more fish than its stomach.

Fish scoop

Pelicans feed by diving, or by dipping their beaks under water. Their beaks have a stretchable pouch used as a fishing net. Pelicans surface with a beakful of fish and seawater. They dribble out the water and gulp down their meal.

Seaside clowns

With their clownlike markings, laughing gulls
are among the most common seaside gulls.
They are named for their noisy call, which
sounds like a crazy laugh.

Takeout food

Some seabirds follow fishing trawlers.
They are not being sociable, just
waiting to scoop up any fish that
fall over the side of the boat.

Feathered but flightless

Not all birds fly, although all have evolved from flying birds. Some, like penguins, walk or hop across rocks. Others such as ostriches, walk or run quickly across the ground.

Can't catch me!

The smaller relatives of ostriches, rheas live in South America, where they avoid predators by running. They run fast with their necks stretched almost level with the ground.

Racing roadrunners

With lightning speed, roadrunners race on foot across the desert after insects, lizards, and snakes. They can even catch and kill rattlesnakes. Roadrunners are able to fly, but prefer to run.

Hop to it

Rockhopper penguins get their name from the way they travel up rocky cliffs. They jump along with their feet together as if taking part in a sack race!

On the run

Ostriches are the tallest and heaviest birds of all. A human being only comes up to the shoulder of a large male ostrich. These giants of the bird world can run as fast as 43 mp/h (70 kmp/h) in short bursts.

Meet the vultures

All members of the vulture family are birds of prey, and their favorite food is carrion – dead and rotting bodies which they scavenge from the ground. They spend most of their lives searching for the next meal!

A featherless head prevents the vulture from getting messy when it feeds.

Designed for life

Vultures, like this white-backed bird, have strong necks and beaks to allow them to tear through the tough skin of prey. They also have excellent eyesight, which allow them to spot victims from a long way off.

THE BLUSHING BIRD

The hooded vulture is a bird that can't easily hide its emotions. When feeling aggressive or excited, the bare skin around its neck and face turns to a dark pink color, as the blood vessels dilate. This may serve to indicate to other vultures what sort of mood the individual bird is in.

High in the sky

The Andean condor is part of the vulture family. One of the largest flying birds in the world, its huge wingspan helps it to glide on warm air-thermals for hours at a time.

Tools for the task

This Egyptian vulture throws rocks at tough ostrich eggs until they crack. It is the only bird of prey known to use a tool in this way.

Disposing of the dead

Most species of vulture feast on a variety of dead animals. A group will clear up a carcass in no time at all, and will often eat so much that it is difficult for them to take to the skies again. Vultures have strong stomachs to cope with rotten and decaying flesh.

Opportunity seekers

Some insect-eating birds have spotted that animals can supply their favorite food. Bird and animal partnerships may benefit both creatures. Other opportunity seekers, like the magpie, help no one but themselves!

Feathered friends

Animals like sheep and cattle often have a bird escort. The animals drive insects from the ground as they feed. Birds called cattle egrets follow the animals to snap up the insects.

Cattle egrets particularly enjoy a meal of grasshoppers, but they are careful to avoid bumblebees and wasps!

A handsome black-and-white bird, the magpie is a member of the crow family.

Nest robber

The common magpie eats almost anything it can find, including insects, small animals, fruit, and seeds. It may even steal eggs or chicks from the nests of smaller birds. It waits until the nest's owners are away before climbing up to the nest and stealing a meal.

Dinner for two

Oxpeckers peck small, bloodsucking parasites, called ticks, out of the skin of large animals like this antelope. The antelope benefits from having these parasites removed, and the birds get a good meal. If oxpeckers spot a predator, such as a lion, they call loudly to warn their host of danger.

An oxpecker may eat hundreds of ticks in one day.

Courtship

Male birds seek to attract females in a variety of ways. Often more decorative than females, the males may show off their feathers. Some give presents of twigs or pieces of food. Others join females in dances, which can take place on the ground, in the water, or in the air.

Fan of feathers

Peacocks open out their "fan," or "train" of feathers in their courtship displays. The peahen is not as colorful as the peacock and lacks his showy tail feather

Puffed up and posing

Male frigate birds have a red throat sac that they can puff up like a huge balloon. They can stay puffed up for hours to catch the eye of a female frigate bird.

Like this frigate bird, male birds often show off to attract females.

Fancy feet

Flashing his feet at a female as he lands, the male blue-footed booby then flaunts his feet in a high-stepping walk. He also brings presents of pieces of nest material.

The finishing touch to the male blue-footed booby's courtship is to tilt his beak to the sky and whistle.

IT TAKES TWO TO TANGO

Some birds dance in pairs during courtship. Cranes perform a dance in which they bow, jump, turn, and perhaps present a twig. Roseate spoonbills may grasp each other's spoon-shaped beaks during their dance. Western grebes dance side by side across water. Eagle pairs perform displays in the air.

Blue bower

To attract females, male bower birds build a shady shelter called a bower on the forest floor. They then decorate this with colorful items. Satin bower birds pick blue objects that match their feathers!

Vivid blue feet and a comical appearance give blue-footed boobies their name.

Nest building

Many birds build nests in high places, like trees or cliffs. Some make their nests on the ground. A bird's nest is its home. Here it can lay eggs and raise chicks, keeping them warm and safe.

Birds on the construction site

To make a nest, birds collect building materials such as grass, mud, and twigs, then push them roughly into place. Some birds sit in the center while they form their nests. Others, like these gray herons, trample their nests into shape.

LUCKY STORKS!

Storks are believed to bring good luck to couples hoping for a baby. It is traditional for villagers in southern Europe to put a wagon wheel on top of their roofs for storks to nest on.

As they shape their nests, gray herons pull twigs into place with their beaks.

Mud hut

Swallows make nests of mud and grass, gluing them on to ledges and walls with mud. They may need to fly a long way to find a stream bank or other mud source.

A redstart has used feathers shed by other birds to insulate its nest for warmth.

Cozy cup nests

Most woodland birds build cup-shaped nests in trees. They may make hundreds of trips to collect materials. They use twigs for structure, adding feathers, seeds, or animal fur for warmth.

Hardworking homemaker

Hanging upside down from a branch, the male weaver bird weaves a balloon-shaped nest. He invites females to inspect it; if one likes the nest she will line it with grass and move in!

Eggs and hatching

A female bird lays eggs, then she or the male bird sits on them to keep them warm. When a chick is ready to hatch, it faces the egg's round end and begins to peck its way through the shell.

Breaking out
A duckling has a special egg tooth, which it uses to break through the eggshell. The tooth falls off once the duckling has hatched.

Protective parent
Like some other birds, emperor geese lay their eggs in nests on the ground. They spend 24 days keeping the eggs warm before their chicks hatch. Parents also have to be on guard to protect their eggs from hungry predators.

Wood thrushes eat fruit, insects, and juicy-looking grubs like these.

Free at last

This tired duckling has spent over a day chipping its way through the shell. Now that it has tumbled out, its feathers are still wet. Soon they will dry out and become fluffy.

Begging beaks

These wood thrush chicks beg for food with their beaks wide open. Until they can fly, they rely on their parents to bring them food. They eat a lot and grow quickly.

Caring for chicks

Parent birds feed their chicks and guard them from harm until they can fend for themselves. Ducklings and some other newly hatched chicks can run, swim, and even find food. Most chicks hatch naked, blind, and helpless.

Free-falling fledglings

Mandarin ducks nest in a hole in a tree, high in the air. When all the eggs are hatched, the mother calls to the chicks from the ground. Each chick crawls out of the hole, launching itself freefall. Amazingly, all the chicks land unhurt. They follow their mother to find food. Mandarin ducks wade and feed in woodland ponds and rocky streams.

Each newly hatched duckling jumps from the tree.

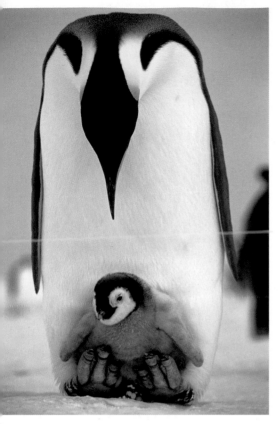

Swanning around

Young swans are called cygnets. With their short necks and fluffy gray feathers, they do not yet look like their beautiful parents. Cygnets can swim, but they may ride on their mother's back!

Keeping cozy

In winter, the female emperor penguin lays a single egg then leaves for the sea. The male holds the egg off the ice on his feet. After the chick hatches, the male keeps it warm until the female returns.

Foster parent

This young cuckoo is larger than the wren feeding it. Cuckoos lay their eggs in other birds' nests. When it hatches, the cuckoo flings out the other eggs. Now it will get all the food.

Globetrotters

Many of the Earth's birds have both a winter and a summer home. In the winter they leave their summer nesting areas, and fly to warmer places where there is more food. This yearly travel is called migration.

A flying flock

Every winter, tens of thousands of snow geese leave their breeding grounds in Canada, and fly approximately 1,200 miles (1,931 km) to California and Mexico. Flying in a "V" formation means that the leader cuts through the air, so that the rest of the flock benefit from a reduction in wind resistance. This makes it much easier to fly.

PACIFIC OCEAN

Canada

snow geese

NORTH AMERICA

ruby-throated hummingbird

Mexico

CENTRAL AMERICA

Arctic

Greenland

EUROPE

arctic tern

ATLANTIC OCEAN

AFRICA

SOUTH
AMERICA

To Antarctica

The farthest of them all
The arctic tern is the real star in the world of migration. Each year it travels an amazing 21,000 miles (35,000 km) around the world, flying from the Arctic to the Antarctic, then back again. It spends most of its life in the air.

Tiny traveler
The ruby-throated hummingbird may be small, but it flies from Canada to Mexico and Central America each year. Here the warm climate and nectar-rich flowers make the 600 mile (1,000 km) journey worthwhile.

Swans on the move
Whooper swans make a yearly migration, traveling to and from locations in Europe and Russia, all the way across to the Pacific coast. These swans fly in large groups by night and day, and rest if visibility becomes poor.

Glossary

Breeding when animals give birth to young.

Camouflage for birds, camouflage is having feathers that match their surroundings in color or pattern. This is to avoid being seen by predators.

Carrion dead, rotting flesh.

Chick a newly hatched young bird.

Colony a group of one kind of bird that lives closely together for a period of time, usually to breed and raise young.

Courtship a process of attracting and impressing a potential mate. In the bird world this may include showing off beautiful feathers, or staging elaborate displays.

Eurasia Europe and Asia.

Evolve all living things change and alter over long periods of time. These changes occur gradually over generations, allowing creatures to adapt to their surroundings.

Flock a group of birds feeding, resting, or traveling together.

Hatch a young bird, or chick, breaking out of its egg.

Gizzard part of a bird's stomach that is used for grinding and crushing food.

Migration the regular seasonal movement of animals from one place to another to find food, a warmer climate or to breed.

Nectar a sugary substance produced by plants to attract insects such as bees, and some birds, such as hummingbirds.

Parasite an animal that lives in, or on, another animal. A parasit benefits at the expense of anoth animal.

Perch a branch or other suppor that birds use to rest on.

Predator an animal that hunts another animal for food.

Prey animals that are hunted b predators for food.

Rain forest a lush, leafy forest i a tropical part of the world wher there is regular heavy rainfall.

Scavenger a bird, or other animal, that eats the remains of an animal that has already been killed.

Songbird a bird with a special voice box that vibrates as it sing A songbird produces more complex sounds than other birds

Species a group of birds or othe animals, or plants, made up of related individuals who are able to produce young with one another.

Territory an area that is defended by a bird, or birds, against others of its kind.

Bird habitats

Every bird featured in this book is
listed here, along with its page
number and where it lives.

Index

Acknowledgments

Dorling Kindersley would like to thank:
Dorian Spencer Davies for original artwork illustrations;
Rose Horridge and Sarah Mills for DK picture library
research; Jacqui Hurst, Barrie Watts and Kim Taylor.

Picture credits:

The publisher would like to thank the following for their
kind permission to reproduce their photographs:
a=above; c=center; b=below; l=left; r=right; t=top;

Aquila Photographics: M.C. Wilkes 11c; Alan Wilson 39r. **BBC
Natural History Unit:** John Cancalosi 10b; Jeff Foot 30cr; Jl Gomez de
Francisco 34tl; Tony Heald 31c; Simon King 17c; Lawrence Michael
10tr; Klaus Nigge 24b; Dietmar Nill 6bl; Jason Smalley 8-9bc. **Bird
World, Surrey:** Frank Greenaway 22bl, 23tr, 23cr. **Bruce Coleman Ltd:**
Erwin and Peggy Bauer 36br; Bruce Coleman Inc 27c, 37c; Kim Taylor
7c, 9cr, 34bl, 39tl; Jorg & Petra Wegner 23bc. **Corbis:** Eric & David
Hosking 8tl, 23cl; Steve Kaufman 28bl; Frank Lane Picture Agency 12bl,

Fritz Polking, 32-33b; Barbra Leigh 25bl; George D. Lepp 38b; Papilio, Robert
Gill 25tc. **Michael & Patricia Fogden:** 21tr. **Chris Gomersall Photography:** 28
29b. **Arthur Morris/Birds As Art:** 8-9b. **Natural History Museum:** 4cr, 4br,
39cl. **N.H.P.A:** Bruce Beehler 20cr; Laurie Campbell 33tr; Stephen Krasemann
45tr; L Hugh Newman 22cr; Rod Planck 30br; Silvestris Fotoservice 17cb; Mirk
Stelzner 22l; Daniel Zupanc 37cr. **Oxford Scientific Films:** Stan Osolinski 14l,
19tr; Maurice Tibbles 43b; Robert A. Tyrrell 5bl; Tom Ulrich 18tl; Konrad
Wothe 44-45b. **Science Photo Library:** Sid Bahrt 36bl; Manfred Danegger 15b
E.R Degginger 15tl; Ken M. Johns 18-19; Stephen J Krasemann 40-41c; George
D. Lepp 12tr; S.R. Maglione 44c; George Ranalli 28-29t; Gregory K Scott 41tr;
Art Wolfe 35c. **Stone, Getty Images:** Art Wolfe 43tl. **Telegraph Colour Librar
Getty Images:** John Lythgoe 36tr. **Vireo:** T.J Ulrich 20tr. **Joanne Williams:** 17t
Windrush Photos: A & E Morris 1c; Arthur Morris 26br; David Tipling 28cr.
Zefa Picture Library: 43tr.

Jacket images: **Ardea London Ltd:** M.Watson back-c. **N.H.P.A.:** Stephen
Dalton tc, bl. **Oxford Scientific Films:** Mark Hamblin bc.

All other images: © Dorling Kindersley. For further information, see
www.dkimages.com